John Henry Newman

The Pope and the Revolution

A Sermon, Preached in the Oratory Church, Birmingham

John Henry Newman

The Pope and the Revolution
A Sermon, Preached in the Oratory Church, Birmingham

ISBN/EAN: 9783337091828

Printed in Europe, USA, Canada, Australia, Japan

Cover: Foto ©Lupo / pixelio.de

More available books at **www.hansebooks.com**

THE

POPE AND THE REVOLUTION:

A SERMON,

PREACHED

IN THE ORATORY CHURCH, BIRMINGHAM,

ON SUNDAY, OCTOBER 7, 1866.

BY

JOHN HENRY NEWMAN, D.D.

LONDON:

LONGMANS, GREEN, READER, AND DYER

1866

Price One Shilling.

THE

POPE AND THE REVOLUTION:

A SERMON,

PREACHED

IN THE ORATORY CHURCH, BIRMINGHAM,

ON SUNDAY, OCTOBER 7, 1866.

BY

JOHN HENRY NEWMAN, D.D.

LONDON:

LONGMANS, GREEN, READER, AND DYER.

1866.

[The right of Translation is reserved.]

ADVERTISEMENT.

This Sermon is given to the world in consequence of its having been made the subject in the public prints of various reports and comments, which, though both friendly and fair to the author, as far as he has seen them, nevertheless, from the necessity of the case, have proceeded from information inexact in points of detail.

It is now published from the copy written beforehand, and does not differ from that copy, as delivered, except in such corrections of a critical nature as are imperative when a composition, written *currente calamo*, has to be prepared for the press. There is one passage, however, which it has been found necessary to enlarge, with a view of expressing more exactly the sentiment which it contained; viz. the comparison made at pp. 43, 44, between Italian and English Catholics.

The author submits the whole, as he does all his publications, to the judgment of Holy Church.

October 13, 1866.

A 2

The Church shone brightly in her youthful days,
 Ere the world on her smiled;
So now, an outcast, she would pour her rays
 Keen, free, and undefiled;
Yet would I not that arm of force were mine,
To thrust her from her awful ancient shrine.

'Twas duty bound each convert-king to rear
 His Mother from the dust;
And pious was it to enrich, nor fear
 Christ for the rest to trust:
And who shall dare make common or unclean,
What once has on the Holy Altar been?

Dear Brothers! hence, while ye for ill prepare,
 Triumph is still your own;
Blest is a pilgrim Church! yet shrink to share
 The curse of throwing down.
So will we toil in our old place to stand,
Watching, not dreading, the despoiler's hand.

       Vid. LYRA APOSTOLICA.

SERMON.

This day, the feast of the Holy Rosary of the Blessed Virgin Mary, has been specially devoted by our ecclesiastical superiors to be a day of prayer for the Sovereign Pontiff, our Holy Father, Pope Pius the Ninth.

His Lordship, our Bishop, has addressed a Pastoral Letter to his clergy upon the subject, and at the end of it he says, " Than that Festival none can be more appropriate, as it is especially devoted to celebrating the triumphs of the Holy See obtained by prayer. We therefore propose and direct that on the Festival of the Rosary, the chief Mass in each church and chapel of our diocese be celebrated with as much solemnity as circumstances will allow of. And that after the Mass the Psalm *Miserere* and the Litany of the Saints be sung or recited. That the faithful be invited to offer one communion for the Pope's intention. And that, where it can be done, one part at least of the Rosary be publicly said at some convenient time in the church, for the same intention."

Then he adds : " In the Sermon at the Mass of the Festival, it is our wish that the preacher should instruct the faithful on their obligations to the Holy See, and on the duty especially incumbent on us at this time of praying for the Pope."

I. " Our obligations to the Holy See." What Catholic can doubt of our obligations to the Holy See ? especially what Catholic under the shadow and teaching of St. Philip Neri can doubt those obligations, in both senses of the word " obligation," the tie of duty and the tie of gratitude ?

1. For first as to duty. Our duty to the Holy See, to the Chair of St. Peter, is to be measured by what the Church teaches us concerning that Holy See and of him who sits in it. Now St. Peter, who first occupied it, was the Vicar of Christ. You know well, my Brethren, our Lord and Saviour Jesus Christ, who suffered on the Cross for us, thereby bought for us the kingdom of heaven. "When Thou hadst overcome the sting of death," says the hymn, " Thou didst open the kingdom of heaven to those who believe." He opens, and He shuts; He gives grace, He withdraws it; He judges, He pardons, He condemns. Accordingly, He speaks of Himself in the Apocalypse as " Him who is the Holy and the True, Him that hath the key of David, (the

key, that is, of the chosen king of the chosen people,) Him that openeth and no man shutteth, that shutteth and no man openeth." And what our Lord, the Supreme Judge, is in heaven, that was St. Peter on earth; he had the keys of the kingdom, according to the text, "Thou art Peter, and upon this rock I will build My Church, and the gates of hell shall not prevail against it. And I will give to thee the keys of the kingdom of heaven; and whatsoever thou shalt bind upon earth, shall be bound also in heaven; and whatsoever thou shalt loose on earth, shall be loosed also in heaven."

Next, let it be considered, the kingdom which our Lord set up with St. Peter at its head was decreed in the counsels of God to last to the end of all things, according to the words I have just quoted, "The gates of hell shall not prevail against it." And again, "Behold, I am with you all days, even to the consummation of the world." And in the words of the prophet Isaias, speaking of that divinely established Church, then in the future, "This is My covenant with them, My Spirit that is in thee, and My words which I have put in thy mouth, shall not depart out of thy mouth, nor out of the mouth of thy seed, nor out of the mouth of thy seed's seed, saith the Lord, from henceforth and for ever." And the prophet Daniel says, "The God of heaven will set up a kingdom that shall never be destroyed . . .

and it shall break in pieces and shall consume all
those kingdoms (of the earth, which went before
it), and itself shall stand for ever."

That kingdom our Lord set up when He came
on earth, and especially after His resurrection;
for we are told by St. Luke that this was His
gracious employment, when He visited the Apostles from time to time, during the forty day's which
intervened between Easter Day and the day of
His Ascension. "He showed Himself alive to
the Apostles," says the Evangelist, "after His
passion by many proofs, for forty days appearing
to them and speaking of the kingdom of God."
And accordingly, when at length He had ascended
on high, and had sent down "the promise of His
Father," the Holy Ghost, upon His Apostles, they
forthwith entered upon their high duties, and
brought that kingdom or Church into shape, and
supplied it with members, and enlarged it, and
carried it into all lands.   As to St. Peter, he
acted as the head of the Church, according to
the previous words of Christ; and, still according to his Lord's supreme will, he at length placed
himself in the see of Rome, where he was martyred.   And what was then done, in its substance
cannot be undone.   "God is not as a man that
He should lie, nor as the son of man, that He
should change.   Hath He said then, and shall He
not do? hath He spoken, and will He not fulfil?"
And, as St. Paul says, "The gifts and the calling

of God are without repentance." His Church then, in all necessary matters, is as unchangeable as He. Its framework, its polity, its ranks, its offices, its creed, its privileges, the promises made to it, its fortunes in the world, are ever what they have been.

Therefore, as it was *in* the world, but not *of* the world, in the Apostles' times, so it is now :— as it was " in honour and dishonour, in evil report and good report, as chastised but not killed, as having nothing and possessing all things," in the Apostles' times, so it is now :—as then it taught the truth, so it does now; as then it had the sacraments of grace, so has it now; as then it had a hierarchy or holy government of Bishops, priests, and deacons, so has it now; and as it had a Head then, so must it have a head now. Who is that visible Head? who is the Vicar of Christ? who has now the keys of the kingdom of heaven, as St. Peter had then? Who is it who binds and looses on earth, that our Lord may bind and loose in heaven? Who, I say, is the successor to St. Peter, since a successor there must be, in his sovereign authority over the Church? It is he who sits in St. Peter's Chair; it is the Bishop of Rome. We all know *this*; it is part of our *faith*; I am not proving it to you, my Brethren. The visible headship of the Church, which was with St. Peter while he lived, has been lodged ever since in his Chair; the successors in his headship are the suc-

cessors in his Chair, the continuous line of Bishops
of Rome, or Popes, as they are called, one after
another, as years have rolled on, one dying and
another coming, down to this day, when we see
Pius the Ninth sustaining the weight of the glorious Apostolate, and that for twenty years past,
—a tremendous weight, a ministry involving mo-
mentous duties, innumerable anxieties, and im-
mense responsibilities, as it ever has done.

And now, though I might say much more about
the prerogatives of the Holy Father, the visible head
of the Church, I have said more than enough for
the purpose which has led to my speaking about
him at all. I have said that, like St. Peter, he is
the Vicar of his Lord. He can judge, and he can
acquit; he can pardon, and he can condemn; he
can command, and he can permit; he can forbid,
and he can punish. He has a supreme jurisdiction
over the people of God. He can stop the ordinary
course of sacramental mercies; he can excom-
municate from the ordinary grace of redemption;
and he can remove again the ban which he has
inflicted. It is the rule of Christ's providence,
that what His Vicar does in severity or in mercy
upon earth, He Himself confirms in heaven. And
in saying all this I have said enough for my purpose, because that purpose is to define our obligations to him. That is the point on which our
Bishop has fixed our attention; "our obligations
to the Holy See;" and what need I say more to

measure our own duty to it and to him who sits in
it, than to say that, in his administration of Christ's
kingdom, in his religious acts, wo must never
oppose his will, or dispute his word, or criti-
cize his policy, or shrink from his side? There
are kings of the earth who have despotic authority, which their subjects obey indeed and disown
in their hearts; but we must never murmur at
that absolute rule which the Sovereign Pontiff has
over us, because it is given to him by Christ, and,
in obeying him, wo are obeying his Lord. We must
never suffer ourselves to doubt, that, in his government of the Church, he is guided by an intelligence
more than human. His yoke is the yoke of Christ,
he has the responsibility of his own acts, not we;
and to his *Lord* must he render account, not to us.
Even in secular matters it is ever safe to be on his
side, dangerous to be on the side of his enemies.
Our duty is, not indeed to mix up Christ's Vicar
with this or that party of men, because he in his
high station is above all parties, but to look at
his acts, and to follow him, whither he goeth, and
never to desert him, however we may be tried, but
to defend him at all hazards, and against all
comers, as a son would a father, and as a wife
a husband, knowing that his cause is the cause
of God. And so, as regards his successors, if we
live to see them; it is our duty to give *them* in
like manner our dutiful allegiance and our un-
feigned service, and to follow them also whither-

soever they go, having that same confidence that
each in his turn and in his own day will do God's
work and will, which we felt in their predecessors,
now taken away to their eternal reward.

2. And now let us consider our obligations to
the Sovereign Pontiff in the second sense, which is
contained under the word "obligation." "In the
Sermon in the Mass," says the Bishop, "it is our
wish that the preacher should instruct the faithful on their obligations to the Holy See;" and
certainly those obligations, that is, the claims of
the Holy See upon our gratitude, are very great.
We in this country owe our highest blessings to
the See of St. Peter,—to the succession of Bishops
who have filled his Apostolic chair. For first it
was a Pope who sent missionaries to this island in
the beginning of the Church, when the island was
yet in pagan darkness. Then again, when our
barbarous ancestors, the Saxons, crossed over
from the Continent and overran the country, who
but a Pope, St. Gregory the First, sent over St.
Augustine and his companions to convert them to
Christianity? and by God's grace they and their
successors did this great work in the course of a
hundred years. From that time, twelve hundred
years ago, our nation has ever been Christian.
And then in the lawless times which followed, and
the break up of the old world all over Europe,
and the formation of the new, it was the Popes,
humanly speaking, who saved the religion of Christ

from being utterly lost and coming to an end, and
not in England only, but on the Continent; that
is, our Lord made use of that succession of His
Vicars, to fulfil His gracious promise, that His
religion should never fail. The Pope and the
Bishops of the Church, acting together in that
miserable time, rescued from destruction all that
makes up our present happiness, spiritual and
temporal. Without them the world would have
relapsed into barbarism—but God willed other-
wise; and especially the Roman Pontiffs, the successors of St. Peter, the centre of Catholic Unity,
the Vicars of Christ, wrought manfully in the
cause of faith and charity, fulfilling in their own
persons the divine prophecy anew, which primarily
related to the Almighty Redeemer Himself: "I
have laid help upon One that is mighty, and I
have exalted One chosen out of the people. I
have found David My servant, with My holy oil
have I anointed him. For My hand shall help him,
and My arm shall strengthen him. The enemy
shall have no advantage over him, nor the son of
iniquity have power to hurt him. I will put to
flight his enemies before his face, and them that
hate him I will put to flight. And My truth
and My mercy shall be with him, and in My Name
shall his horn be exalted. He shall cry out to Me,
Thou art my Father, my God, and the support of
my salvation. And I will make him My first-born,
high above the kings of the earth. I will keep

My mercy for him for ever, and My covenant shall be faithful to him."

And the Almighty did this in pity towards His people, and for the sake of His religion, and by virtue of His promise, and for the merits of the most precious blood of His own dearly-beloved Son, whom the Popes represented. As Moses and Aaron, as Josue, as Samuel, as David, were the leaders of the Lord's host in the old time, and carried on the chosen people of Israel from age to age, in spite of their enemies round about, so have the Popes from the beginning of the Gospel, and especially in those middle ages when anarchy prevailed, been faithful servants of their Lord, watching and fighting against sin and injustice and unbelief and ignorance, and spreading abroad far and wide the knowledge of Christian truth.

Such they have been in every age, and such are the obligations which mankind owes to them; and, if I am to pass on to speak of the present Pontiff, and of our own obligations to him, then I would have you recollect, my Brethren, that it is he who has taken the Catholics of England out of their unformed state and made them a Church. He it is who has redressed a misfortune of nearly three hundred years' standing. Twenty years ago we were a mere collection of individuals; but Pope Pius has brought us together, has given us Bishops, and created out of us a body politic, which (please God), as time goes on, will play an important part in Christendom, with a character, an intellect, and a power of its own, with schools of its own, with a definite influence in the counsels of the Holy Church Catholic, as England had of old time.

This has been his great act towards our country; and then specially, as to his great act towards us here, towards me. One of his first acts after he was Pope was, in his great condescension, to call me to Rome; then, when I got there, he bade me send for my friends to be with me; and he formed us into an Oratory. And thus it came to pass that, on my return to England, I was able to associate myself with others who had not gone to Rome, till we were so many in number, that not only did we establish our own Oratory here, whither the Pope had specially sent us, but we found we could throw off from us a colony of zealous and able priests into the metropolis, and establish there, with the powers with which the Pope had furnished me, and the sanction of the late Cardinal, that Oratory which has done and still does so much good among the Catholics of London.

Such is the Pope now happily reigning in the chair of St. Peter; such are our personal obligations to him; such has he been towards England, such towards us, towards you, my Brethren. Such he is in his benefits, and, great as are the claims of those benefits upon us, great equally are the claims on us of his personal character and of his many virtues. He is one whom to see is to love; one who overcomes even strangers, even enemies, by his very look and voice; whose presence subdues, whose memory haunts, even the sturdy resolute mind of the English Protestant. Such is the Holy Father of Christendom, the worthy successor of a long and glorious line. Such is he; and, great as he is in office, and in his beneficent acts and virtuous life, as great is he in the severity of his trials, in the complication of his duties, and in the gravity of his perils,—perils, which are at this moment closing him in on every side; and therefore it is, on account of the crisis of the long-protracted troubles of his Pontificate which seems near at hand, that our Bishop has set apart this day for special solemnities, the Feast of the Holy Rosary, and has directed us to "instruct the faithful on their *obligations* to the Holy See," and not only so, but also " on the duty especially incumbent on us at this time of *praying* for the Pope."

II. This then is the second point to which I have to direct your attention, my Brethren—the duty of praying for the Holy Father; but, before doing so, I must tell you what the Pope's long-protracted troubles are about, and what the crisis is, which seems approaching :—I will do it in as few words as I can.

More than a thousand years ago, nay near upon

fifteen hundred, began that great struggle, which
I spoke of just now, between the old and the new
inhabitants of this part of the world. Whole
populations of barbarians overran the whole face
of the country, that is, of England, France, Ger-
many, Spain, Italy, and the rest of Europe. They
were heathens, and they got the better of the
Christians; and religion seemed likely to fail together with that old Christian stock. But, as I
have said, the Pope and the Bishops of the Church
took heart, and set about converting the new
comers, as in a former age they had converted
those who now had come to misfortune; and,
through God's mercy, they succeeded. The Saxon
English,—Anglo-Saxons, as they are called,—are
among those whom the Pope converted, as I said
just now. The new convert people, as you may
suppose, were very grateful to the Pope and
Bishops, and they showed their gratitude by
giving them large possessions, which were of
great use, in the bad times that followed, in maintaining the influence of Christianity in the world.
Thus the Catholic Church became rich and powerful. The Bishops became princes, and the Pope
became a Sovereign Ruler, with a large extent of
country all his own. This state of things lasted
for many hundred years; and the Pope and
Bishops became richer and richer, more and more
powerful, until at length the Protestant revolt
took place, three hundred years ago, and ever

since that time, in a temporal point of view, they
have become of less and less importance, and less
and less prosperous. Generation after generation
the enemies of the Church, on the other hand,
have become bolder and bolder, more powerful,
and more successful in their measures against the
Catholic faith. By this time the Church has well-
nigh lost all its wealth and all its power; its
Bishops have been degraded from their high places
in the world, and in many countries have scarcely
more, or not more, of weight or of privilege than
the ministers of the sects which have split off
from it. However, though the Bishops lost, as
time went on, their temporal rank, the Pope did not
lose his; he has been an exception to the rule ; according to the Providence of God, he has retained
Rome, and the territories round about Rome, far
and wide, as his own possession without let or
hindrance. But now at length, by the operation
of the same causes which have destroyed the
power of the Bishops, the Holy Father is in
danger of losing his temporal possessions. For the
last hundred years he has had from time to time
serious reverses, but he recovered his ground. Six
years ago he lost the greater part of his dominions,
—all but Rome and the country immediately about
it,—and now the worst of difficulties has occurred
as regards the territory which remains to him.
His enemies have succeeded, as it would seem, in
persuading at least a large portion of his subjects

to side with them.   This is a real and very trying
difficulty.   While his subjects are for him, no
one can have a word to say against his temporal
rule; but who can force a Sovereign on a people
which deliberately rejects him?   You may attempt
it for a while, but at length the people, if they
persist, will get their way.

They give out then, that the Pope's government
is behind the age,—that once indeed it was as good
as other governments, but that now other governments have got better, and his has not,—that he can
neither keep order within his territory, nor defend
it from attacks from without,—that his police and
his finances are in a bad state,—that his people
are discontented within,—that he does not show
them how to become rich,—that he keeps them
from improving their minds,—that he treats them
as children,—that he opens no career for young
and energetic minds, but condemns them to in-
activity and sloth,—that he is an old man,—that
he is an ecclesiastic,—that, considering his great
spiritual duties, he has no time left him for temporal concerns,—and that a bad religious government is a scandal to religion.

I have stated their arguments as fairly as I can,
but you must not for an instant suppose, my
Brethren, that I admit either their principles or
their facts.   It is a simple paradox to say that
ecclesiastical and temporal power cannot lawfully,
religiously, and usefully be joined together.   Look

at what are called the middle ages,—that is, the
period which intervenes between the old Roman
Empire and the modern world; as I have said, the
Pope and the Bishops saved religion and civil order
from destruction in those tempestuous times,—and
they did so *by means* of the secular power which they
possessed.   And next, going on to the principles
which the Pope's enemies lay down as so very
certain, who will grant to them, who has any pre-
tension to be a religious man, that progress in
temporal prosperity is the greatest of goods, and
that every thing else, however sacred, must give
way before it ?   On the contrary, health, long life,
security, liberty, knowledge, are certainly great
goods, but the possession of heaven is a far greater
good than all of them together.   With all the
progress in worldly happiness which we possibly
could make, we could not make ourselves im-
mortal,—death must come; that will be a time
when riches and worldly knowledge will avail us
nothing, and true faith, and divine love, and a past
life of obedience will be all in all to us.   If we
were driven to choose between the two, it would
be a hundred times better to be Lazarus in this
world, than to be Dives in the next.

However, the best answer to their arguments
is contained in sacred history, which supplies us
with a very apposite and instructive lesson on the
subject, and to it I am now going to refer.

Now observe in the first place, no Catholic

maintains that that rule of the Pope as a king, in Rome and its provinces, which men are now hoping to take from him, is, strictly speaking, what is called a Theocracy, that is, a Divine Government. His government, indeed, in spiritual matters, in the Catholic Church throughout the world, might be called a Theocracy, because he is the Vicar of Christ, and has the assistance of the Holy Ghost; but not such is his kingly rule in his own dominions. On the other hand, the rule exercised over the chosen people, the Israelites, by Moses, Josue, Gideon, Eli, and Samuel, *was* a Theocracy: God *was* the king of the Israelites, *not* Moses and the rest,—*they* were but Vicars or Vicegerents of the Eternal Lord who brought the nation out of Egypt. Now, when men object that the Pope's government of his own States is not what it should be, and that therefore he ought to lose them, because, forsooth, a religious rule should be perfect or not at all, I take them at their word, if they are Christians, and refer them to the state of things among the Israelites after the time of Moses, during the very centuries when they had God for their king. Was that a period of peace, prosperity, and contentment? Is it an argument against the Divine Perfections, that it was not such a period? Why is it then to be the condemnation of the Popes, who are but men, that their rule is but parallel in its characteristics to that of the

King of Israel, who was God? He indeed has His
own all-wise purposes for what He does; He
knows the end from the beginning; He could
have made His government as perfect and as
prosperous as might have been expected from the
words of Moses concerning it, as perfect and
prosperous as, from the words of the Prophets,
our anticipations might have been about the earthly
reign of the Messias. But this He did not do,
because from the first He made that perfection
and that prosperity dependent upon the free will,
upon the co-operation of His people. Their loyal
obedience to Him was the condition, expressly
declared by Him, of His fulfilling His promises.
He proposed to work out His purposes *through*
them, and, when they refused their share in the
work, every thing went wrong. Now they did
refuse from the first; so that from the very first,
He says of them emphatically, they were a " stiffnecked people." This was at the beginning of
their history; and close upon the end of it, St.
Stephen, inspired by the Holy Ghost, repeats the
divine account of them: "You stiffnecked and
uncircumcised in heart and ears, you always resist
the Holy Ghost; as your fathers did, so do you
also." In consequence of this obstinate disobe-
dience, I say, God's promises were not fulfilled to
them. That long lapse of five or six hundred
years, during which God was their King, was in

good part a time, not of well-being, but of calamity.

Now, turning to the history of the Papal monarchy for the last thousand years, the Roman people have not certainly the guilt of the Israelites, because they were not opposing the direct rule of God; and I would not attribute to them now a liability to the same dreadful crimes which stain the annals of their ancestors; but still, after all, they have been a singularly stiffnecked people in time past, and in consequence, there has been extreme confusion, I may say anarchy, under the reign of the Popes; and the restless impatience of his rule which exists in the Roman territory now, is only what has shown itself age after age in times past. The Roman people not seldom offered bodily violence to their Popes,—killed some Popes, wounded others, drove others from the city. On one occasion they assaulted the Pope at the very altar in St. Peter's, and he was obliged to take to flight in his pontifical vestments. Another time they insulted the clergy of Rome; at another, they attacked and robbed the pilgrims who brought offerings from a distance to the shrine of St. Peter. Sometimes they sided with the German Emperors against the Pope; sometimes with other enemies of his in Italy itself. As many as thirty-six Popes endured this dreadful contest with their own subjects, till at last, in anger and disgust with Rome and Italy, they took refuge in France, where they remained for seventy years, during the reigns of eight of their number[1].

That I may not be supposed to rest what I have said on insufficient authorities, I will quote the words of that great Saint, St. Bernard, about the Roman people, seven hundred years ago.

Writing to Pope Eugenius during the troubles of the day, he says, "What shall I say of the people? why, that it *is* the Roman people. I could not more concisely or fully express what I think of your subjects. What has been so notorious for ages as the wantonness and haughtiness of the Romans? a race unaccustomed to peace, accustomed to tumult; a race cruel and unmanageable up to this day, which knows not to submit, unless when it is unable to make fight. . . . I know the hardened heart of this people, but God is powerful even of these stones to raise up children to Abraham. . . . Whom will you find for me out of the whole of that populous city, who received you as Pope without bribe or hope of bribe? And then especially are they wishing to be masters, when they have professed to be servants. They promise to be trustworthy, that they may have the opportunity of injuring those who trust them. . . . They are wise for evil, but they are ignorant

[1] I take these facts as I find them in Gibbon's History, the work which I have immediately at hand; but it would not be difficult to collect a multitude of such instances from the original historians of those times.

for good. Odious to earth and heaven, they have assailed both the one and the other; impious towards God, reckless towards things sacred, factious among themselves, envious of their neighbours, inhuman towards foreigners, . . . they love none, and by none are loved. Too impatient for submission, too helpless for rule ; . . . importunate to gain an end, restless till they gain it, ungrateful when they have gained it. They have taught their tongue to speak big words, while their performances are scanty indeed *."

Thus I begin, and now let us continue the parallel between the Israelites and the Romans.

I have said that, while the Israelites had God for their King, they had a succession of great national disasters, arising indeed really from their falling off from Him ; but this they would have been slow to acknowledge. They fell into idolatry ; then, in consequence, they fell into the power of their enemies ; then God in His mercy visited them, and raised up for them a deliverer and ruler, —a Judge, as he was called,—who brought them to repentance, and then brought them out of their troubles ; however, when the Judge died, they fell back into idolatry, and then they fell under the power of their enemies again. Thus for eight years they were in subjection to the King of Mesopotamia ; for eighteen years to the King of Moab ; for twenty years to the King of Canaan ; for seven

* De Consid. iv. 2. Vide note at the end.

years to the Madianites; for eighteen years to the Ammonites; and for forty years to the Philistines. Afterwards Eli, the high priest, became their judge, and then disorders of another kind commenced. His sons, who were priests also, committed grievous acts of impurity in the holy place, and in other ways caused great scandal. In consequence a heavy judgment came upon the people; they were beaten in battle by the Philistines, and the Ark of God was taken. Then Samuel was raised up, a holy prophet and a judge, and in the time of his vigour all went well; but he became old, and then he appointed his sons to take his place. They, however, were not like him, and every thing went wrong again. "His sons walked not in his ways," says the sacred record, "but they turned aside after lucre, and took bribes, and perverted judgment." This reduced the Israelites to despair; they thought they never should have a good government, while things were as they were; and they came to the conclusion that they had better not be governed by such men as Samuel, however holy he might be, that public affairs ought to be put on an intelligible footing, and be carried on upon system, which had never yet been done. So they came to the conclusion that they had better have a king, like the nations around them. They deliberately preferred the rule of man to the rule of God. They did not like to repent and give up their sins, as the true means of being prosperous; they thought it an easier way to temporal prosperity to have a king like the nations, than to pray and live virtuously. And not only the common people, but even the grave and venerable seniors of the nation took up this view of what was expedient for them. "All the ancients of Israel, being assembled, came to Samuel, ... and they said to him ... Make us a king to judge us, as all nations have." Observe, my Brethren, this is just what the Roman people are saying now. They wish to throw off the authority of the Pope, on the plea of the disorders which they attribute to his government, and to join themselves to the rest of Italy, and to have the King of Italy for their king. Some of them, indeed, wish to be without any king at all; but, whether they wish to have a king or no, at least they wish to get free from the Pope.

Now let us continue the parallel. When the prophet Samuel heard this request urged from such a quarter, and supported by the people generally, he was much moved. "The word was displeasing in the eyes of Samuel," says the inspired writer, "that they should say, Give us a king. And Samuel prayed to the Lord." Almighty God answered him by saying, "They have not rejected thee, but Me;" and He bade the prophet warn the people, what the king they sought after would be to them, when at length they had him. Samuel accordingly put before them explicitly

what treatment they would receive from him.
" He will take your sons," he said, " and will put
them in his chariots; and he will make them his
horsemen, and his running footmen to go before
his chariots. He will take the tenth of your corn
and the revenues of your vineyards. Your flocks
also he will take, and you shall be his servants."
Then the narrative proceeds, "But the people would
not hear the voice of Samuel, and they said, Nay,
but there shall be a king over us. And we also will
be like all nations, and our king shall judge us, and
go out before us, and fight our battles for us."

Now here the parallel I am drawing is very
exact. It is happier, I think, for the bulk of a
people, to belong to a small State which makes
little noise in the world, than to a large one. At
least in this day we find small states, such as
Holland, Belgium, and Switzerland, have special
and singular temporal advantages. And the Roman people, too, under the sway of the Popes, at
least have had a very easy time of it; but, alas,
that people is not sensible of this, or does not
allow itself to keep it in mind. The Romans have
not had those civil inconveniences, which fall so
heavy on the members of a first-class Power. Tho
Pontifical Government has been very gentle with
them; but, if once they were joined to the kingdom of Italy, they would at length find what it is
to attain temporal greatness. The words of Samuel
to the Israelites would be fulfilled in them to the

letter. Heavy taxes would bo laid on them; their
children would bo torn from them for the army;
and they would incur tho other penalties of an
ambition which prefers to havo a sharo in a political adventuro to being at the head of Catholic
citizenship. Wo cannot havo all things to our
wish in this world; we must take our choice
between this advantago and that; perhaps the
Roman peoplo would like both to securo this world
and tho next, if they could; perhaps, in seeking
both, they may loso both; and perhaps, when they
havo lost moro than they have gained, they may
wish their old Sovereign back again, as they have
dono in other centuries beforo this, and may regret
that they have caused such grievous disturbanco
for what at length they find out is little worth it.

In truth, after all, the question which they have
to determine is, as I have intimated, not one of
worldly prosperity and adversity, of greatness or
insignificance, of despotism or liberty, of position in
tho world or in the Church; but a question of
spiritual life or death. The sin of tho Israelites
was not that they desired good government, but
that they rejected God as their King. Their
choosing to have " a king like the nations " around
them was, in matter of fact, the first step in a
series of acts, which at length led them to their
rejection of the Almighty as their God. When
in spite of Samuel's remonstrances they were
obstinate, God let them have their way, and then

in time they became dissatisfied with their king
for the very reasons which the old. Prophet had set
before them in vain. On Solomon's death, about
a hundred and twenty years after, the greater part
of the nation broke off from his son on the very
plea of Solomon's tyranny, and chose a new king,
who at once established idolatry all through their
country.

Now, I grant, to reject the Holy Father of
course is not the sin of the Israelites, for they rejected Almighty God Himself: yet I wish I was
not forced to believe that a hatred of the Catholic
Religion is in fact at the bottom of that revolutionary spirit which at present seems so powerful
in Rome. Progress, in the mouth of some people,—
of a great many people,—means apostasy. Not
that I would deny that there are sincere Catholics
so dissatisfied with things as they were in Italy,
as they are in Rome, that they are brought to think
that no social change can be for the worse. Nor
as if I pretended to be able to answer all the ob-
jections of those who take a political and secular
view of the subject. But here I have nothing to
do with secular politics. In a sacred place I have
only to view the matter religiously. It would ill
become me, in my station in the Church and my
imperfect knowledge of the facts of the case, to
speak for or against statesmen and governments,
lines of policy or public acts, as if I were invested
with any particular mission to give my judgment, or

had any access to sources of special information. I have not here to determine what may be politically more wise, or what may be socially more advantageous, or what in a civil point of view would work more happily, or what in an intellectual would tell better; my duty is to lead you, my Brethren, to look at what is happening, as the sacred writers would now view it and describe it, were they on earth now to do so, and to attempt this by means of the light thrown upon present occurrences by what they actually have written whether in the Old Testament or the New.

We must remove, I say, the veil off the face of events, as Scripture enables us to do, and try to speak of them as Scripture interprets them for us. Speaking then in the sanctuary, I say that theories and schemes about government and administration, be they better or worse, and the aims of mere statesmen and politicians, be they honest or be they deceitful, these are not the determining causes of that series of misfortunes under which the Holy See has so long been suffering. There is something deeper at work than any thing human. It is not any refusal of the Pope to put his administration on a new footing, it is not any craft or force of men high in public affairs, it is not any cowardice or frenzy of the people, which is the sufficient explanation of the present confusion. What it is our duty here to bear in mind, is the constant restless agency over the earth of that bad angel who was a liar from the beginning, of whom Scripture speaks so much. The real motive cause of the world's troubles is the abiding presence in it of the apostate spirit, " The prince of the power of this air," as St. Paul calls him, " The spirit that now worketh on the children of unbelief."

Things would go on well enough but for him. He it is who perverts to evil what is in itself good and right, sowing cockle amid the wheat. Advance in knowledge, in science, in education, in the arts of life, in domestic economy, in municipal administration, in the conduct of public affairs, is all good and from God, and might be conducted in a religious way; but the evil spirit, jealous of good, makes use of it for a bad end. And much more able is he to turn to his account the designs and measures of worldly politicians. He it is who spreads suspicions and dislikes between class and class, between sovereigns and subjects, who makes men confuse together things good and bad, who inspires bigotry, party spirit, obstinacy, resentment, arrogance and self-will, and hinders things from righting themselves, finding their level, and running smooth. His one purpose is so to match, and arrange, and combine, and direct the opinions and the measures of Catholics and unbelievers, of Romans and foreigners, of sovereigns and popular leaders—all that is good, all that is bad, all that is violent or lukewarm in the good, all that is morally great and intellectually persuasive in the bad—as to inflict the widest possible damage, and utter ruin, if that were possible, on the Church of God.

Doubtless in St. Paul's time, in the age of heathen persecution, the persecutors had various good political arguments in behalf of their cruelty. Mobs indeed, or local magistrates, might be purposely cruel towards the Christians; but the great Roman Government at a distance, the great rulers and wise lawyers of the day, acted from views of large policy; they had reasons of State, as the kings of the earth have now; still our Lord and His Apostles do not hesitate to pass these by, and declare plainly that the persecution which they sanctioned or commanded was the work, not of man, but of Satan. And now in like manner we are not engaged in a mere conflict between progress and reaction, modern ideas and new, philosophy and theology, but in one scene of the never-ending conflict between the anointed Mediator and the devil, the Church and the world; and, in St. Paul's words, "we wrestle not against flesh and blood, but against principalities and powers, against the world-rulers of this darkness, against the spirits of wickedness in the high places."

Such is the Apostle's judgment, and how, after giving it, does he proceed? "Therefore," he says, "take unto you the armour of God, that you may be able to resist in the evil day and to stand in all things perfect. Stand therefore, having

c

your loins girt about with truth, and having on the breast-plate of justice, and your feet shod with the preparation of the gospel of peace; in all things taking the shield of faith, whereby you may be able to quench all the fiery darts of the wicked. And take unto you the helmet of salvation and the sword of the Spirit, which is the Word of God." And then he concludes his exhortation with words which most appositely bear upon the point towards which all that I have been saying is directed,—"praying at all times with all prayer and supplication in the spirit, and watching therein with all instance and supplication for all the Saints, and for me," that is, for the Apostle himself, "that speech may be given me, that I may open my mouth with confidence to make known the mystery of the Gospel."

Here, then, we are brought at length to the consideration of the duty of prayer for our living Apostle and Bishop of Bishops, the Pope. I shall attempt to state distinctly what is to be the *object* of our prayers for him, and, secondly, what the *spirit* in which we should pray, and so I shall bring my remarks on this great subject to an end.

1. In order to ascertain the exact *object* of our prayers at this time, we must ascertain what is the *occasion* of them. You know, my Brethren, and I have already observed, that the Holy Father has been attacked in his temporal possessions again and again in these last years, and we have

all along been saying prayers daily in the Mass in his behalf. About six years ago the northern portion of his States threw off his authority. Shortly after, a large foreign force, uninvited, as it would seem, by his people at large,—robbers I will call them,—(this is not a political sentiment, but an historical statement, for I never heard any one, whatever his politics, who defended their act in itself, but only on the plea of its supreme expedience, of some State necessity, or some theory of patriotism,)—a force of sacrilegious robbers,— broke into provinces nearer to Rome by a sudden movement, and, without any right except that of the stronger, got possession of them, and keeps them to this day.[1] Past outrages, such as these, are never to be forgotten; but still they are not the occasion, nor do they give the matter, of our present prayers. What that occasion, what that object is, we seem to learn from his Lordship's letter to his clergy, in which our prayers are required. After speaking of the Pope's being "stripped of part of his dominions," and "deprived of all the rest, with the exception of the marshes and deserts that surround the Roman capital," he fastens our attention on the fact, that "now at last is the Pope to be left standing alone, and standing face to face with those unscrupulous adversaries, whose boast and whose vow to all the world it is, not to leave to him one single foot of Italian ground except

[1] Vide Note at the end.

c 2

beneath their sovereign sway." I understand, then, that the exact object of our prayers is, that the territory still his should not be violently taken from him, as have been those larger portions of his dominions of which I have already spoken.

This too, I conceive, is what is meant by praying for the Holy See. "The duty of every true child of Holy Church," says the Bishop, "is to offer continuous and humble prayer for the Father of Christendom, and for the protection of the Holy See." By the Holy See we may understand Rome, considered as the seat of Pontifical government. We are to pray for Rome, the see, or seat, or metropolis of St. Peter and his successors. Further, we are to pray for Rome as the seat, not only of his spiritual government, but of his temporal. We are to pray that he may continue king of Rome; that his subjects may come to a better mind; that, instead of threatening and assailing him, or being too cowardly to withstand those who do, they may defend and obey him; that, instead of being the heartless tormentors of an old and venerable man, they may pay a willing homage to the Apostle of God; that, instead of needing to be kept down year after year by troops from afar, as has been the case for so long a time, they may, "with a great heart and a willing mind," form themselves into the glorious body-guard of a glorious Master; that they may obliterate and expiate what is so great a scandal to the

world, so great an indignity to themselves, so
great a grief to their Father and king, that
foreigners are kinder to him than his own flesh
and blood; that now at least, though in the end
of days, they may reverse the past, and, after the
ingratitude of centuries, may unlearn the pattern
of that rebellious people, who began by rejecting
their God and ended by crucifying their Redeemer.

2. So much for the *object* of our prayers;
secondly, as to the *spirit* in which we should pray.
As we ever say in prayer "Thy will be done," so
we must say now. We do not absolutely know
God's will in this matter; we know indeed it is
His will that we should ask; we are not absolutely sure that it is His will that He should
grant. The very fact of our praying shows that
we are uncertain about the event. We pray when
we are uncertain, not when we are certain. If we
were quite sure what God intended to do, whether
to continue the temporal power of the Pope or to
end it, we should not pray. It is quite true
indeed that the event may *depend upon* our prayer,
but by such prayer is meant perseverance in prayer
and union of prayers; and we never can be certain that this condition of numbers and of fervour
has been sufficiently secured. We shall indeed
gain our prayer if we pray enough; but, since it
is ever uncertain what *is* enough, it is ever uncertain what will be the event. There are Eastern
superstitions, in which it is taught that, by means

of a certain number of religious acts, by sacrifices, prayers, penances, a man of necessity extorts from God what he wishes to gain, so that he may rise to supernatural greatness even against the will of God. Far be from us such blasphemous thoughts! We pray to God, we address the Blessed Virgin and the Holy Apostles and the other guardians of Rome, to defend the Holy City; but we know the event lies absolutely in the hands of the Allwise, whose ways are not as our ways, whose thoughts are not as our thoughts, and, unless we had been furnished with a special revelation on the matter, to be simply confident or to predict would be presumption. Such is Christian prayer; it implies hope and fear. We are not certain we shall gain our petition, we are not certain we shall not gain it. Were we certain that we should not, we should give ourselves to resignation, not to prayer; were we certain we should, we should employ ourselves, not in prayer, but in praise and thanksgiving. While we pray then in behalf of the Pope's temporal power, we contemplate both sides of the alternative, his retaining it, and his losing it; and we prepare ourselves both for thanksgiving and resignation, as the event may be. I conclude by considering each of these issues of his present difficulty.

(1.) First, as to the event of his retaining his temporal power. I think this side of the alternative (humanly speaking) to be highly probable.

I should be very much surprised if in the event he did not keep it. I think the Romans will not be able to do without him;—it is only a minority even now which is against him; the majority of his subjects are not wicked, so much as cowardly and incapable. Even if they renounce him now for a while, they will change their minds and wish for him again. They will find out that he is their real greatness. Their city is a place of ruins, except so far as it is a place of holy shrines. It is the tomb and charnel-house of pagan impiety, except so far as it is sanctified and quickened by the blood of martyrs and the relics of saints. To inhabit it would be a penance, were it not for the presence of religion. Babylon is gone, Memphis is gone, Persepolis is gone; Rome would go, if the Pope went. Its very life is the light of the sanctuary. It never could be a suitable capital of a modern kingdom without a sweeping away of all that makes it beautiful and venerable to the world at large. And then, when its new rulers had made of it a trim and brilliant city, they would find themselves on an unhealthy soil and a defenceless plain. But, in truth, the tradition of ages and inveteracy of associations make such a vast change in Rome impossible. All mankind are parties to the inviolable union of the Pope and his city. His autonomy is a first principle in European politics, whether among Catholics or Protestants; and where can it be secured so well as in that city, which has so long been the seat of its exercise? Moreover, the desolateness of Rome is as befitting to a kingdom which is not of this world as it is incompatible with a creation of modern political theories. It is the religious centre of millions all over the earth, who care nothing for the Romans who happen to live there, and much for the martyred Apostles who so long have lain buried there; and its claim to have an integral place in the very idea of Catholicity is recognized not only by Catholics, but by the whole world.

It is cheering to begin our prayers with these signs of God's providence in our favour. He expressly encourages us to pray, for before we have begun our petition, He has begun to fulfil it. And at the same time, by beginning the work of mercy *without* us, He seems to remind us of that usual course of His providence, viz. that He means to finish it *with* us. Let us fear to be the cause of a triumph being lost to the Church, because we would not pray for it.

(2.) And now, lastly, to take the other side of the alternative. Let us suppose that the Pope loses his temporal power, and returns to the condition of St. Sylvester, St. Julius, St. Innocent, and other great Popes of early times. Are we therefore to suppose that he and the Church will come to nought? God forbid! To say that the Church can fail, or the See of St. Peter can fail, is to deny the faithfulness of Almighty God to His

word. "Thou art Peter, and upon this rock
will I build my Church, and the gates of hell shall
not prevail against it." To say that the Church
cannot live except in a particular way, is to make
it "subject to elements of the earth." The Church
is not the creature of times and places, of temporal
politics or popular caprice. Our Lord maintains
her by means of this world, but these means are
necessary to her only while He gives them; when
He takes them away, they are no longer necessary. He works by means, but He is not
bound to means. He has a thousand ways of
maintaining her; He can support her life, not by
bread only, but by every word that proceedeth out
of His mouth. If He takes away one defence, He
will give another instead. We know nothing of
the future: our duty is to direct our course according to our day; not to give up of our own
act the means which God has given us to main-
tain His Church withal, but not to lament over
their loss, when He has taken them away. Temporal power has been the means of the Church's
independence for a very long period; but, as her
Bishops have lost it a long while, and are not the
less Bishops still, so would it be as regards her
Head, if he also lost his. The Eternal God is her
refuge, and as He has delivered her out of so
many perils hitherto, so will He deliver her still.
The glorious chapters of her past history are but
anticipations of other glorious chapters still to

come. See how it has been with her from the
very beginning down to this day. First, the
heathen populations persecuted her children for
three centuries, but she did not come to an end.
Then a flood of heresies was poured out upon her,
but still she did not come to an end. Then the
savage tribes of the North and East came down
upon her and overran her territory, but she did
not come to an end. Next, darkness of mind,
ignorance, torpor, stupidity, reckless corruption,
fell upon the holy place, still she did not come to
an end. Then the craft and violence of her own
strong and haughty children did their worst against
her, but still she did not come to an end. Then
came a time when the riches of the world flowed
in upon her, and the pride of life, and the refine-
ments and the luxuries of human reason; and lulled
her rulers into an unfaithful security, till they
thought their high position in the world would
never be lost to them, and almost fancied that it
was good to enjoy themselves here below;—but
still she did not come to an end. And then came
the so-called Reformation, and the rise of Protestantism, and men said that the Church had dis-
appeared and they could not find her place. Yet,
now three centuries after that event, *has*, my Brethren, the Holy Church come to an end ? has Protestantism weakened her powers, terrible enemy
as it seemed to be when it arose ? has Protestantism, that bitter energetic enemy of the Holy See,

harmed the Holy See? Why, there never has been a time, since the first age of the Church, when there has been such a succession of holy Popes, as since the Reformation. Protestantism has been a great infliction on such as have succumbed to it; but it has even wrought benefits for those whom it has failed to seduce. By the mercy of God it has been turned into a spiritual gain to the members of Holy Church.

Take again Italy, into which Protestantism has not entered, and England, of which it has gained possession :—now I know well that, when Catholics are good in Italy, they are very good ; I would not deny that they attain there to a height and a force of saintliness of which we seem to have no specimens here. This, however, is the case of souls, whom neither the presence nor the absence of religious enemies would affect for the better or the worse. Nor will I attempt the impossible task of determining the amount of faith and obedience among Catholics respectively in two countries so different from each other. But, looking at Italian and English Catholics externally and in their length and breadth, I may leave any Protestant to decide, in which of the two there is at this moment a more demonstrative faith, a more impressive religiousness, a more generous piety, a more steady adherence to the cause of the Holy Father. The English are multiplying religious buildings, decorating churches, endowing monasteries, educat-

ing, preaching, and converting, and carrying off in
the current of their enthusiasm numbers even of
those who are external to the Church ; the Italian
statesmen, on the contrary, in our Bishop's words,
"imprison and exile the bishops and clergy, leave the
flocks without shepherds, confiscate the Church's
revenues, suppress the monasteries and convents,
incorporate ecclesiastics and religious in the army,
plunder the churches and monastic libraries, and
expose Religion herself, stripped and bleeding in
every limb, the Catholic Religion in the person of
her ministers, her sacraments, her most devoted
members, to be objects of profane and blasphemous
ridicule." In so brave, intelligent, vigorous-
minded a race as the Italians, and in the 19th
century not the 16th, and in the absence of any
formal protest of classes or places, the act of the
rulers is the act of the people. At the end of
three centuries Protestant England contains more
Catholics who are loyal and energetic in word and
deed, than Catholic Italy. So harmless has been
the violence of the Reformation ; it professed to
eliminate from the Church doctrinal corruptions,
and it has failed both in what it has done and in
what it has not done ; it has bred infidels, to its
confusion ; and, to its dismay, it has succeeded in
purifying and strengthening Catholic commu-
nities.

It is with these thoughts then, my Brethren,
with these feelings of solemn expectation, of joyful

confidence, that we now come before our God, and
pray Him to have mercy on His chosen Servant,
His own Vicar, in this hour of trial. We come to
Him, like the prophet Daniel, in humiliation for
our own sins and the sins of our kings, our princes,
our fathers, and our people in all parts of the
Church; and therefore we say the *Miserere* and
the Litany of the Saints, as in a time of fast.
And we come before Him in the bright and glad
spirit of soldiers who know they are under the
leading of an Invincible King, and wait with beat-
ing hearts to see what He is about to do; and
therefore it is that we adorn our sanctuary, bring-
ing out our hangings and multiplying our lights, as
on a day of festival. We know well we are on the
winning side, and that the prayers of the poor,
and the weak, and despised, can do more, when
offered in a true spirit, than all the wisdom and
all the resources of the world. This seventh of
October is the very anniversary of that day
on which the prayers of St. Pius, and the Holy
Rosary said by thousands of the faithful at his
bidding, broke for ever the domination of the
Turks in the great battle of Lepanto. God will
give us what we ask, or He will give us something
better. In this spirit let us proceed with the
holy rites which we have begun,—in the presence
of innumerable witnesses, of God the Judge of all,
of Jesus the Mediator of the New Covenant, of
His Mother Mary our Immaculate Protectress, of

all the Angels of Holy Church, of all the blessed
Saints, of Apostles and Evangelists, Martyrs and
Confessors, holy preachers, holy recluses, holy
virgins, of holy innocents taken away before actual
sin, and of all other holy souls who have been
purified by suffering, and have already reached
their heavenly home.

NOTES.

NOTE I., on p. 25.

St. Bernard is led to say this to the Pope in consequence of
the troubles created in Rome by Arnald of Brescia." Ab obitu
Cælestini hoc anno invalescere cœpit istiusmodi rebellio Romanorum adversus Pontificem, eodemque hæresis dicta Politicorum,
sive Arnaldistarum. Ea erant tempora infelicissima, cùm Ro-
mani ipsi, quorum fides in universo orbe jam à tempore Aposto-
lorum annunciata semper fuit, resilientes modo à Pontifice,
dominandi cupidine, ex filiis Petri et discipulis Christi, fiunt
soboles et alumni pestilentissimi Arnaldi de Brixiâ. Verùm,
cùm tu Romanos audis, ne putes omnes eâdem insaniâ percitos,
nam complures ex nobilium Romanorum familiis, iis relictis, pro
Pontifice rem agebant, &c." Baron. Annal. in ann. 1144. 4.

NOTE II., on p. 35.

The following Telegram in the *Times* of September 13, 1860,
containing Victor Emmanuel's formal justification of his in-
vasion and occupation of Umbria and the Marches in a time
of peace, is a document for after times:—

Turin, Sept. 11, evening.

The King received to-day a deputation from the inhabitants
of Umbria and the Marches.

His Majesty granted the protection which the deputation
solicited, and orders have been given to the Sardinian troops to
enter those provinces by the following Proclamation:—

"Soldiers! You are about to enter the Marches and Umbria, in order to establish civil order in the towns now desolated by misrule, and to give to the people the liberty of expressing their own wishes. You will not fight against the armies of any of the Powers, but will free those unhappy Italian provinces from the bands of foreign adventurers which infest them. You do not go to revenge injuries done to me and Italy, but to prevent the popular hatred from unloosing itself against the oppressors of the country.

"By your example you will teach the people forgiveness of offences, and Christian tolerance to the man who compared the love of the Italian fatherland to Islamism.

"At peace with all the great Powers, and holding myself aloof from any provocation, I intend to rid Central Italy of one continual cause of trouble and discord. I intend to respect the seat of the Chief of the Church, to whom I am ever ready to give, in accordance with the allied and friendly Powers, all the guarantees of independence and security, which his misguided advisers have in vain hoped to obtain for him from the fanaticism of the wicked sect which conspires against my authority and against the liberties of the nation.

"Soldiers! I am accused of ambition. Yes; I have one ambition, and it is to re-establish the principles of moral order in Italy, and to preserve Europe from the continual dangers of revolution and war."

The next day the Times, in a leading article, thus commented on the above:—

"Victor Emmanuel has in Garibaldi a most formidable competitor. . . . [Piedmont] must therefore, at whatever cost or risk, make herself once more mistress of the revolution. She must lead, that she may not be forced to follow. She must revolutionize the Papal States, in order that she may put herself in a position to arrest a dangerous revolutionary movement against Venetia. . . . These motives are amply sufficient to account for the decisive movement of Victor Emmanuel. He lives in revolutionary times, when self-preservation has superseded all other considerations, and it would be childish to apply to his situation the maxims of international law which are applicable to periods of tranquillity.

" These being the motives which have impelled Piedmont to draw the sword, we have next to see what are the grounds on which she justifies the step. These grounds are two,—the extraordinary misrule and oppression of the Papal Government, and the presence of large bands of foreign mercenaries, by which the country is oppressed and terrorized. The object is said to be to give the people an opportunity of expressing their own wishes and the re-establishment of civil order. The king promises to respect the seat of the Chief of the Church,—Rome, we suppose, and its immediate environs; but, while holding out this assurance, the manifesto speaks of the Pope and his advisers in terms of bitterness and acrimony unusual in the present age, even in a declaration of war. He will teach the people forgiveness of offences, and Christian tolerance to the Pope and his general. He denounces the misguided advisers of the Pontiff, and the fanaticism of the wicked sect which conspires against his authority and the liberties of the nation. This is harsh language, and is not inconsistently seconded by the advance into the States of the Church of an army of 50,000 men."

It was the old Fable of the Wolf and the Lamb.

THE END.

GILBERT AND RIVINGTON, PRINTERS, ST. JOHN'S SQUARE, LONDON.